The different kinds of tree

There are five different kinds of tree. The conifers and the broadleaved trees are the most well-known; the cycads, gingkoes and tree ferns are quite rare. Conifers covered most of the world in prehistoric times. Dinosaurs brushed up against their needle-like leaves as they passed. Today, conifers live only in the cooler places. Broadleaved trees are the most common kind of tree everywhere else.

Leaves

Conifers and broadleaved trees have quite different kinds of leaves. Conifers have long, pointed leaves called needles, or small, flat ones called scales. They can survive in harsh weather. Broadleaved trees have wide, thin leaves which catch a lot of light but cannot survive without warmth and water.

Seeds

One of the main differences between conifers and broadleaved trees is the way their seeds develop. The seeds of conifers grow in cones. When the cone opens its scales, the seeds fall out. They are no longer protected. The seeds of broadleaved trees are often protected inside a hard nut or fleshy fruit, even after they have fallen from the tree.

Evergreen and deciduous

Conifers are evergreen. This means that they do not shed all of their leaves at once at any one time of the year. Their old leaves are constantly replaced by new ones. Broadleaved trees are evergreen in countries where there is plenty of warmth and water all year round. In countries that have cold winters, they shed their leaves in autumn. Trees that do this are known as deciduous trees. The leaves turn red, brown and yellow before they fall. This changes the colour of the forest.

The shape of broadleaved trees

Broadleaved trees tend to spread out as they grow. This is so that their broad, flat leaves can catch as much light as possible. A tree growing on its own will spread out to its fullest size and shape. In a wood, the trees tend to grow taller and thinner in their search for light.

Elm   Beech

The shape of coniferous trees

Many conifers tend to grow upward rather than outward. Some, such as the Norway spruce, have a conical shape. Others fill out at the top, or crown.

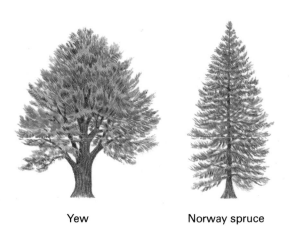

Yew   Norway spruce

The gingko tree

The gingko tree is a survivor from prehistoric times. Fossils of its leaves show that it has not changed for 200 million years. For a long time, people thought that gingkoes no longer grew in the wild. In this century, however, they were found growing in China.

The cycads

The rare cycads grow in tropical and sub-tropical countries. They are short, fat trees but they grow enormous cones that weigh up to 36 kilograms.

Tree ferns

Tree ferns grow in the rain forests of Australia and New Zealand. They have trunks of closely packed fibres.

Palms

Palms are a kind of broadleaved tree. The trunk is not like that of an ordinary tree; it consists of leaf-bases tightly packed together. If you were to cut through the trunk, you would not see rings as you would in a conifer or broadleaved tree.

Discovering trees

You can make a study of the trees in your area. Make sketches of the overall shape of the tree, of the leaves, buds, seeds and the texture of the bark. When you have made a note of these features, it will be easier to find out the name of the tree from a good identification guide.

A tree's life cycle

Fully grown trees produce seeds that grow into saplings. These saplings grow into trees and produce seeds, and so on. The birth and growth of new trees is a never-ending cycle. What happens in the cycle, and when, depends on the amount of water there is and the temperature.

The maple tree shown far right lives in a country that has cold winters and warm summers, a temperate country. Its life cycle is affected by the temperature and amount of light.

The seeds of the maple fall to the earth in late summer. They must get away from the parent tree, for they cannot grow in 'second-hand soil' or in deep shade.

1 The seeds can only start to grow or germinate when the temperature is right and if there is enough water. In this country that means it has to wait until next spring. The first thing to appear is a rootlet called the radicle. This anchors the seed to the soil.

2 The radicle pushes its way deeper into the soil and begins to absorb water and minerals.

3 A stem begins to grow upwards. In some kinds of tree, the stem actually lifts the seed case off the ground. Side roots now grow from the radicle.

4 Seed leaves then open out. These leaves begin to absorb sunlight and produce food for the seedling's growth.

5 A shoot emerges between the seed leaves. This carries leaves which look like small versions of the adult tree's leaves.

6 Later, the seedling will produce buds on the tips and at the sides of its shoots. The side buds will eventually become branches. The original stem will carry on growing upwards.

7 As the seedling grows, layers of woody tissue will be added to the stem. The stem will become a strong and rigid trunk to support the tree. When it is fully grown, the tree will produce seeds of its own.

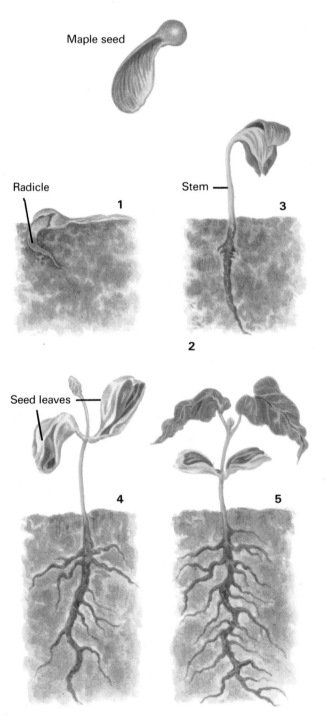

Maple seed

Radicle

Stem

1

3

2

Seed leaves

4

5

Seed facts

- A fully grown oak tree will produce 50 000 seeds, or acorns, in the late summer. It needs to; a single wood pigeon will eat 140 acorns in a day.
- The seeds of *Eucalyptus regnans* are as small as particles of dust, but they grow into trees that are 100 metres high.
- Forest fires are a natural occurrence in some parts of Australia. The seeds of some Australian trees cannot start to grow unless they've been burnt in a fire.

How trees grow

Trees grow in two different ways. At the tip of each twig is a bud which grows shoots to make the tree taller and wider. At the same time, the branches and the trunk get fatter. They need to become stronger to support the weight of the new growth at the tips.

Growth rings

In temperate climates, deciduous trees do most of their growing in spring and summer. The trunk thickens because it produces a new layer of cells called cambium cells. The new cambium forms rings in the trunk, a pale one for spring and a dark one in summer. It is possible to work out the age of a tree by counting the rings.

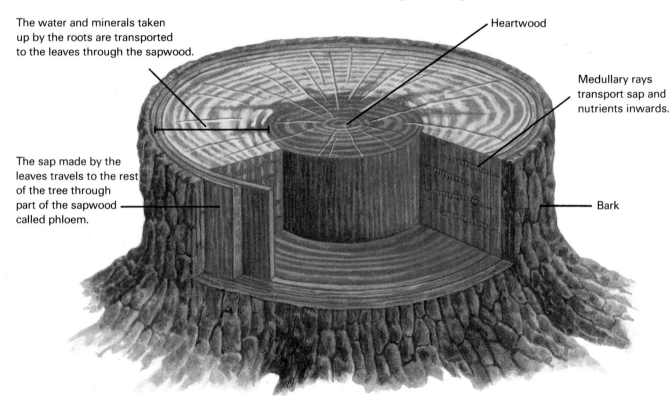

The water and minerals taken up by the roots are transported to the leaves through the sapwood.

Heartwood

Medullary rays transport sap and nutrients inwards.

The sap made by the leaves travels to the rest of the tree through part of the sapwood called phloem.

Bark

Transport systems

In the branches and trunk there are two different kinds of wood: heartwood and sapwood. Heartwood is made up of dead cells and supports the tree. Sapwood has vessels through which minerals, water and sap can travel around the tree.

The flow of water and minerals happens in the outer layers of the trunk and branches. Although the heartwood supports the tree, it can survive without it. This is why you see hollow trees living and flourishing as normal.

Measuring the age of a tree

Trees living in temperate countries, like England, add about 2.5 centimetres to the circumference of their trunks every year. You can use this information to estimate the age of a tree. Measure the circumference of the trunk in centimetres about 1.5 metres from the ground. Divide this number by 2.5 to get the age of the tree. Remember that this is a very rough estimate. The growth of trees varies from one species to another and from one year to another.

Taking root

The roots of a tree grow outwards to a distance that matches the height of the tree. They have two jobs to do. They prevent the tree from falling over by anchoring it to the soil, and they absorb water and minerals.

Setting up home

Roots bind the soil together. They prevent it from slipping or being washed away. Animals such as rabbits and badgers often make their homes among the roots of trees. The roots absorb the water from the soil so that their burrows stay dry. They also prevent the burrows from collapsing.

Mangrove survival

Waterlogged soil is too unstable to support a tree. It also lacks oxygen. Mangrove trees have developed special roots to cope with the mud-flats in which they live. Stilt roots help to support them in the shifting soil. Breathing roots rise up out of the mud into the air above.

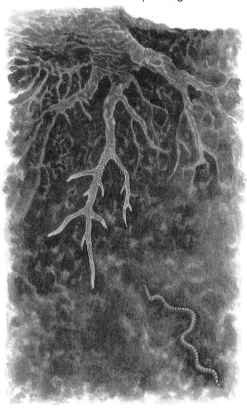

The tip of a root has a strong cap to prevent wear and tear as it forces its way through the soil.

The burrows made by earthworms let air into the soil around the roots.

Leaves

The leaves produce food for the whole tree, but they can only do this in the light. The leaves are shaped and arranged and held up by the branches so that they can catch as much sunlight as possible.

Budding into life

Leaves begin life as buds. Growth stops in the winter, but the buds contain all that is needed for rapid growth as soon as it gets warmer. The bud at the tip of the twig often contains flowers as well as leaves. The side buds carry only leaves.

Inside a horse chestnut bud

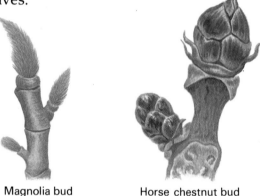

Magnolia bud   Horse chestnut bud

Protected buds

Some trees have buds that are protected by thick scales. Others are covered in a thick fur or are sticky. The aim is to protect the leaves and flowers inside from hungry animals and damp.

Designer leaves

The leaves of broadleaved trees come in two designs: simple and compound. A simple leaf grows from the twig on its own stalk. Compound leaves are made up of several leaflets on a stalk. Each compound leaf grows from a single bud and falls off in one piece in the autumn.

Oak   Snake-bark maple   Japanese maple

Simple leaves

Making food

Trees do not go in search of food; they make their own by means of photosynthesis. The leaves take carbon dioxide (CO_2) from the air and water from the soil. Using the energy they get from the sun, they make sugars from these two ingredients. This food keeps the tree alive. Oxygen (O) is given off during photosynthesis. Since all animals need oxygen to survive, it's easy to see why we need trees.

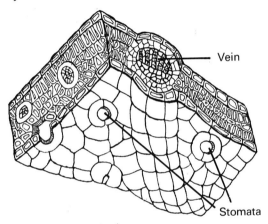

Vein

Stomata

Inside a leaf

The picture below left shows the structure of a leaf from a broadleaved tree. The stomata let carbon dioxide and oxygen in and out of the leaf. They also control the amount of water lost. Nutrients are transported through the leaf in the veins.

Water loss experiment

You can prove that trees take up water and lose it through their leaves in this simple experiment. Take a beaker and half fill it with water. Make a mark where the water level is. Add a small amount of cooking oil. This will float on the water. Place a cutting from a tree into the beaker and leave for a few days. The water level will have dropped. The water could not have evaporated through the oil, so it must have been lost through the leaves of the cutting.

Rowan or Mountain ash

Ash

Compound leaves

Horse chestnut

Pollination

Pollination happens when male cells, or pollen, fall on to the female stigma. If they are of the same kind of tree, the pollen grows a tube. When this reaches the ovule, fertilization takes place, and the seed develops.

Wind pollination
Most of the trees which grow in temperate countries are pollinated by the wind. The pollen comes from male flowers that are separate from the female flowers. The wind carries the pollen between them.

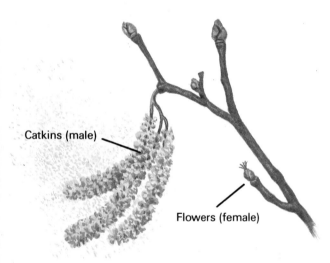

Catkins (male)

Flowers (female)

Catkins
The hazel catkins grow in the autumn, but they do not release their pollen until the following spring. Each catkin releases into the air a fine dust of over two million pollen grains. These attach themselves to the sticky stigma of the female flower.

Flowers first
Most trees have male and female flowers that grow on the same tree. Some produce their flowers before the leaves grow. This stops the leaves getting in the way of pollination.

Insect pollination
The flowers of wind-pollinated trees are small and hard to see. Insect-pollinated trees have flowers that are brightly coloured and scented to attract the insects. They also produce a sweet sugar-rich food just for the insects; this is the nectar.

The male and female parts grow on a single flower. Pollination happens when pollen from the anthers of one flower is transferred by an insect to the stigma of another flower. The flower cannot fertilize itself.

Birds and bats
It is not just insects that pollinate flowers. In the tropics, bats and birds also transfer pollen as they feed on the energy-rich nectar.

Apple blossom – insect-pollinated

Fruits, berries and seeds

Trees have evolved many different ways of scattering their seeds far and wide to suitable growing places. Most of them produce as many seeds as possible, so some are bound to survive.

Tasty fruit

Many trees produce seeds that are inside a soft, juicy fruit or berry. The fruit is eaten by birds and animals, but the seeds are hard. They cannot be digested, and are passed out with the animals' droppings. By this time, the animal may be a long way from the parent tree and the seeds grow into new trees which are not overshadowed by the parent.

Secret food stores

Squirrels gather nuts in the autumn and bury them as food stores for winter. Quite often, the squirrel forgets where the store is. The nuts are in the soil some distance from the parent tree – just where they need to be to grow!

Blowing in the wind

Willow seeds are covered in fluffy fibres. They are picked up by the wind and carried away.

Floating away

Trees that live on coasts or river banks use the water to carry away their seeds. The seed of the coconut palm floats out to sea and may travel for many months. Many of them sink, but some reach land and germinate.

A fire-tailed sunbird eating nectar

Life in a tree

A single tree provides food and shelter for a huge number of creatures, many of which never leave the tree during their lifetime. It is their natural home or habitat. In a woodland, a tree is just a small part of a larger habitat.

A full-grown oak tree, such as the one shown here, may be home to 300 different types of insect. These insects are food for birds and mammals. Nearly every part of the tree is lived in by something.

Moth larvae

The leaves of the tree are eaten by the young, or larvae, of many kinds of insect. This larva is the caterpillar of a Tortrix moth.

Spangle galls

The spangle galls shown here contain the larvae of Cynips wasps. In the summer, they fall from the tree and the larvae develop in the dead leaves below.

Marble galls

Marble galls are formed by the tree as a reaction against the larvae of the gall wasp. The larvae live and feed safely inside the gall.

Bark beetle

The bark of the tree is supposed to protect the sapwood beneath. It is home to many kinds of insects. This beetle bores tunnels through the trunk.

Woodpeckers feed on insects found in the bark.

Rabbit

Jays feed on acorns and help to distribute them.

Squirrels live and feed in the branches of trees.

Rabbits, mice and shrews live in burrows among the roots.

Shrew   Mouse

Leaf litter dwellers

All leaves, whether they belong to an evergreen or a deciduous tree, eventually die and fall to the ground. Here bacteria and fungi feed on them and turn them into leaf litter. Millipedes, woodlice and springtails live here. The leaf litter finally breaks down completely and the nutrients in it are returned to the soil.

Millipede   Woodlouse   Springtail

Life in the forests

Trees are not supposed to live alone. They naturally form forests. The plants and animals that live in forests need each other to survive. Over time, a balance of life has evolved. This is easily upset. The disappearance of one species can mean disaster for others.

The rain forests

The tropical rain forests of South America, Asia and Africa have been around for millions of years. Lots of sunlight and water make these areas perfect places for trees.

The plants and trees of the rain forests grow in layers. Each layer has its own level of light and humidity, and its own kinds of animals. These animals are well-suited to the layer in which they live and cannot live anywhere else.

Rain forest facts
- There is a greater variety of life in the rain forests than anywhere else on Earth. Fifty per cent of the world's species of living things are found in them.
- There are about 100 different kinds of tree in every hectare of rain forest.
- The rain forests of Madagascar have over four times as many trees as the whole of North America.

Emergent layer. Some trees break through the canopy to reach heights of up to 60 metres.

Canopy layer. Most of the sunlight is absorbed by the thic covering of leaves at this layer.

Many rain forest plants live on the branches of the trees. Earthworms live in the leaf litter these plants produce, and frogs live on their moist leaves. All this happens hundreds of metres above the ground.

Understorey

Shrub layer

Herb layer. Plants living here must be able to grow in deep shade.

Lesser anteater

On the forest floor, insects such as termites eat dead plant and animal remains that fall from above.

Quetzal bird

Opossum

Pygmy marmosets eat sap from the trunks of the trees.

Snakes in the canopy eat small birds and mammals.

Sloths eat leaves high up in the canopy.

Spider monkeys move swiftly through the canopy layer.

Toucan

Amazing rain forests

- Cannon Ball trees produce huge, heavy seeds that crash through the canopy layer to reach the ground below.
- Sloths have microscopic green plants growing in their fur. This makes them hard to see among the green leaves.
- A male hornbill collects about 24 000 fruits to feed the female while she looks after the eggs and chicks.

Trees and the climate

Earth is a large and varied planet. To help us study the Earth, we divide it up into smaller areas, called ecosystems. Each ecosystem has its own weather patterns or climate. It also has its own set of plants and animals which are used to the climate.

Trees everywhere

Trees can be found in every ecosystem on land, except for the coldest and the hottest ones. They have features which enable them to cope with the weather of the region in which they live.

Trees in place

This map shows where in the world the different kinds of tree can be found.

- **CONIFEROUS FORESTS**
- **TEMPERATE BROADLEAVED FORESTS**
- **TROPICAL FORESTS**

Shedding snow

Fir, spruce and pine are coniferous trees that live in cold places. Their branches bend without breaking under the weight of snow. When the branches are low, the snow slips off the smooth, waxy leaves.

Storing water

The baobab tree lives in parts of Africa where it is hot and dry for long periods. When the rains come, the baobab stores water in its thick trunk. Later, the trunk shrinks as the tree uses up the water.

Dropping leaves

Being deciduous is a reaction to the climate. Broadleaved trees grow thin, wide leaves to catch a lot of sunlight. In winter the water in the ground is frozen and the tree's sap cannot flow. The tree can no longer feed its leaves, so it drops them and waits until next spring to grow some more.

Drip tips

In the rain forests, it rains almost every day. The leaves of some rain forest trees are waxy with pointed tips. Water runs easily off a leaf shaped like this. If it didn't, the huge trees would become waterlogged and collapse.

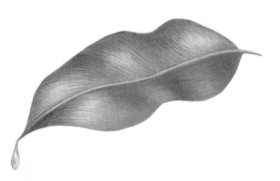

Thick leaves

Eucalyptus trees live in Australia, in places that are often hot and dry. The leaves are tough and leathery. This stops them from drying out in the hot winds and scorching sun.

Lying low

Trees and plants that grow on the cold windswept sides of mountains are often short and close to the ground. This is because there is little water and only a thin layer of soil. Also, the cold winds would soon kill a tall, spreading tree.

Reach for the sky

When a dead rain forest tree or animal decays, its nutrients go straight into the root systems of the trees. The soil contains few nutrients. For this reason, rain forest trees do not push their roots deep into the soil. Instead, they grow thick buttress roots above the soil which help to support their great height.

People and the forests

Few people live and work in temperate forests the way they used to, but people still live in the tropical rain forests. The forests provide them with food, clothes and shelter.

Living in the forest

It is not easy to move quietly and quickly through thick vegetation and animals can be difficult to see. There are many dangerous insects and reptiles. Forest tribes live by clearing small areas of forest to grow crops and keep animals. They also hunt and fish, and gather fruit and nuts.

The hunter's skill

Many forest people are skilled at hunting animals and gathering food. They can identify thousands of different kinds of plants and know when they will bear fruit. This Indian is hunting with a poison-dart blowpipe.

Yanomani Indians on their way to a feast

Rain forest harvest

There are many different kinds of food in the rain forest. These include nuts, berries, fruit, young leaves and shoots, roots and tubers, honey from wild bees, fish, birds, rats, squirrels and lizards.

A slash and burn area in Indonesia

Slash and burn

Many tribes live by clearing small areas of forest to plant crops. They stay in one place for between one and three years, and then move on. This is called 'shifting cultivation' or 'slash and burn', because they slash back the vegetation and burn it to clear an area in which to live.

Nothing is wasted

Once a site has been chosen, the fruit is gathered. Timber from large trees is used to make homes. Small trees and shrubs are burnt. The ashes put valuable nutrients into the poor soil.

Large trees are cut down to allow light to reach the ground below and to provide timber. The tree cutter is raised above the thick buttress roots on a platform. A few large trees are sometimes left for religious reasons.

Planting crops

Rain forest tribes do not need many gardening tools. The soil is easily worked. Holes for the seeds are made with a stick. As the crop grows, so do the weeds. In time, so many weeds grow that the tribe moves on. The patch slowly becomes overgrown and returns to the forest it was before. Because only small patches are cleared, no great damage is done to the forest.

Using wood

From the earliest times, the wood from trees has been used for fuel and for making things. In some parts of the world it is still one of the most important materials. In other areas the lack of forests and the development of materials such as plastic mean that less wood is used than before.

A world of wood

A hundred years ago people in Britain used wood to make many everyday things. Different kinds of wood have different qualities and uses, but they all have some things in common: they are easy to shape, long-lasting and good to look at.

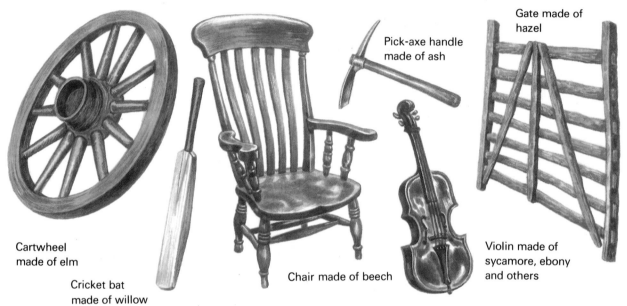

Cartwheel made of elm

Cricket bat made of willow

Chair made of beech

Pick-axe handle made of ash

Violin made of sycamore, ebony and others

Gate made of hazel

A sixteenth century timber-framed house

Wooden home

In the past, many houses were made with a strong timber frame. This was common in parts of the country where there were large forests. The oak beams of this house are joined together with thick, wooden pins. It is possible to take the house apart and build it somewhere else like redoing a jigsaw puzzle.

Rain forest furniture

The European furniture makers of the eighteenth century wanted wood from the rain forests that their countrymen had just discovered. This fashion for tropical woods began the destruction of the rain forests that still goes on today.

H.M.S. Victory, Lord Nelson's flagship

Pollarding a willow tree

Shipbuilding

Wood is ideal for making boats. It is easily shaped and it floats. The earliest boats were probably canoes cut from a single trunk. The most spectacular wooden ships were the ships-of-the-line built in the eighteenth century. These massively timbered ships used the wood of 2000 trees, that's 60 acres of woodland.

Managing trees

Harvesting trees doesn't always mean cutting them down. Pollarding, shown left, is an old method. The main branches of the tree are cut and made into fences and poles. The tree grows new branches which can be harvested every seven years. Coppicing means cutting the tree at ground level. Hazel is coppiced to make hurdles or fences.

From timber to wood

In the past, the hard work of producing useful wood from the forest was done by human and horse power. Today, machinery makes the job easier. More trees can be cut down in less time.

1 In the past, all tree felling was carried out with axe and hand saw. Felling is skilled work. The tree must fall in the right direction without damaging others.

2 Today, petrol-driven saws make felling work easier. In countries where this machinery is not available, the foresters still use hand saws and axes.

3 Horses were once used to pull logs on to carts and out of the forest.

4 Today's foresters use large machinery to remove the timber.

5 Vast numbers of logs can be carried to the sawmills by river. In the past, men were employed to follow the logs and free them when they jammed.

6 In the past, the large trunks were cut with long two-handled saws. One man stood above the trunk and another stood below it in a saw pit.

7 Today, large mechanized saws cut the trunks and logs into planks in a fraction of the time it used to take. Now, as then, very little wood is wasted.

Working with wood

People who work with wood divide wood into two types: hardwood and softwood. Generally, hardwood comes from broadleaved trees and softwood from conifers. These names are misleading. Yew is classified as a softwood, but it is very hard. In fact, it is so dense that it sinks in water.

For centuries the different kinds of wood have been used for making different things. Oak has been used in house building for centuries.

In the past, ash was used for making spears and tool handles. It was also used in carriage building. Today it is used to make furniture.

Cherry wood changes colour from slightly pink to deep red as it ages. It is used to make high-class furniture and ornamental boxes.

Walnut can be shaped easily. It sometimes has a swirling pattern which makes it popular with cabinet makers.

Oak

Cherry

Ash

Walnut

Working with wood

Carpenters are people who take timber and use it to make roofs, floors, window frames, staircases and furniture. Carpentry is an ancient skill. The wood is planed first to make it smooth.

Turning wood

Wood can be cut into rounded shapes as it turns in a lathe. Turned wood is used to make the legs of chairs and tables and banisters in staircases.

Pushing and pulling

In western countries, we make saws that cut as you push them away from you into the wood. Planes work in the same way. In Japan, carpenters use saws and planes which cut as they are pulled back towards the body.

A cabinet maker at work

Carving

Carving is one of the oldest ways of decorating and making things. The carver uses tools such as chisels and gouges to shape the wood. A skilled carver always follows the direction of the grain; this prevents the wood from breaking or splitting. Oak, teak and mahogany are popular with carvers because they are strong and last a long time. Lime and sycamore are fine grained and can be carved into patterns with lots of detail.

A wooden totempole from Alaska

Religious art

Woodcarving is important in many cultures. Many different kinds of people carve images of their gods and decorate their temples and churches with carvings.

Modern art

Sculptors also use wood for non-religious art. The wood is often carved and polished in such a way that the pattern of the grain is an important part of the finished work.

Miniature trees

Bonsai is an ancient form of art from Japan. Bonsai trees are real trees that remain miniature because they are given only a small amount of soil and water. They are highly prized and many become family heirlooms.

A cherrywood sculpture

Topiary

The ancient Romans started an art form now known as topiary. Evergreen trees and hedges are clipped into shapes such as pyramids, spirals or even peacocks with spreading tails.

Wood as fuel

Since the earliest times, people have used wood for making homes, tools and means of transport. Wood also provides us with energy to cook our food and heat our homes.

The energy crisis

In Europe, the large forests were cut down a long time ago. There is no longer enough wood to supply our needs. We still use the fossil fuels oil, coal and gas, but we have to find new sources of energy.

Gathering wood

Two-thirds of the people living in Africa, India and parts of China still depend on wood for fuel. Where the forests are being cut down, it is becoming harder to find wood. Collecting firewood takes up more and more time, because people are having to walk many miles each day to find it. It is often women who collect firewood. These women are Kayapó Indians from the Amazon rain forest in South America.

A prehistoric forest, from which coal was formed

A coal miner at work

Fossil fuels

Coal is found deep below the surface of the earth. It was formed from forests of ferns, mosses and giant horsetails which lived millions of years ago. These trees died and fell to the ground. They were squashed under layers of rock. The heat and pressure turned them into layers of coal called seams.

Energy from the ground

In Britain, about 100 000 000 tonnes of coal are removed from the ground every year. It is used to make electricity to provide energy for our homes and factories. One day it will run out. In the meantime, the more we use, the more we will pollute our air.

Charcoal

Charcoal is a fuel made by heating wood to high temperatures over a long period. The wood is not fully burnt, but most of its moisture is removed. Charcoal was once used to make iron, for drying hops to make beer and for making gunpowder. Today we use it for lighting barbecues, because it burns without smoke.

The charcoal burner

Making charcoal is a skilled craft. In the past, many men lived in the forests making charcoal. They piled the wood up and covered it with turf. Then it was burnt slowly for five days and nights.

A charcoal burner

Tree products

Wood is not the only valuable product that comes from trees. The bark, sap and fruits of many trees can also be harvested. The good thing about these products is that you don't have to cut down the tree to get them.

Cork

Cork is the bark of the evergreen cork oak which grows in Spain and Portugal. It is one of the few trees that does not die when its bark is removed. The bark can be cut away every ten to fifteen years.

Resin

Conifers produce a sticky substance called resin. This protects them from damage and damp. Resin is collected from the trunks of the trees and used to make rosin and turpentine.

Book of bark

Bark was once used for writing on. The words were scratched on to it with a sharp tool. In some countries, people used bark even after paper was invented because it was cheaper.

Rubber

Natural rubber is made from latex. This is the sap of certain trees which grow in Africa and South America. Slanting cuts are made in the bark of the tree. The white latex oozes out of these cuts and collects in a small cup. The rubber industry was once bigger business than it is now. Artificial rubbers are now made, but in the Amazon hundreds of thousands of people still earn their living in this way.

Treasures of the rain forest

The Amazonian Indians know how to use 1000 different kinds of plant from their rain forest home. They use them for building, making clothes, food and medicines. It has been worked out that the fruits and other products from the rain forest are worth more money than timber. If they are harvested carefully, the forests can go on producing them for ever.

Medicine from the trees

The Amazonian Indians use over 100 plants to make their medicines. Some of these plants are used to make medicines for people all over the world. Western scientists have studied only a few of them. It may be that there are many more cures waiting to be discovered in the rain forests.

Brazilian Indians weave baskets and mats from palms that grow in the forest.

Rattan

Rattan is a climbing plant found in the rain forests of Asia. Its stem is very strong and is used to make rope, baskets and furniture. It is a valuable crop for some countries, but can only be produced if the forests stay as they are.

Did you know?

- Sixty per cent of the world's population depends on medicines that are made in the traditional way from plants and trees.
- There are 1650 tropical rain forest plants that could be used to grow valuable crops.
- One Amazonian tree has sap that is so like diesel oil it can be used to run a truck.
- Resins and latexes from some trees can also be used to make perfumes, cable insulation and fillings for teeth.

A rattan cutter from the Philippines in south-east Asia

Food from trees

An apple orchard

Trees gradually developed fruit as a way of spreading their seeds. Humans have devised ways of making syrup from sap and spices from bark, but fruit is still the main food we get from trees.

Selecting the best

Wild apples are small and bitter to taste. Over several centuries, people have bred trees that grow large, sweet apples that are good to eat. This has been done by collecting seeds from the best trees, and by cross-breeding one tree with another so that their offspring produce a better apple.

There are a thousand different kinds of cultivated apple. The trees are bred not only to produce as many apples as possible, but also to be shorter, which makes the picker's job easier.

Cox

Crispin

Egremont Russet

Food from sap

Maple syrup comes from the sap of the sugar maple tree. The sap is tapped from the trunk of the tree without doing it any damage. It is then concentrated by boiling into the syrup we can use on pancakes, waffles and ice-cream.

Chocolate tree

Chocolate is made from the beans of the cocoa tree, shown below. The beans grow inside large fruits. The Aztecs who lived in South America hundreds of years ago were the first people to make chocolate. They used the beans as a form of money, and only rich people could afford to drink chocolate.

Collecting maple sap

Spicy bark

The spice cinnamon, which we use to flavour desserts, is made from the bark of a tree that grows in India. The bark is cut from young saplings.

Fungus harvest

Shiitake is an edible fungus that grows on the wood of the golden chestnut tree. In Japan, stacks of this wood are used as 'beds' on which to grow the fungus.

Pig food

Acorns are a favourite food of pigs. In the past, farmers used to let their pigs into woodlands in the autumn so that they could have a feast.

The fruits of the cocoa tree

Paper

Paper is one of the world's most important materials. It is hard to imagine life without it. Some paper is made from cotton and linen fibres, some from recycled used paper, but most of it is made from wood. About half the world's timber production goes to make paper.

Newspaper plantations

It takes 5000 trees to make enough paper for just one edition of a large daily newspaper. Huge forests of fast-growing trees such as eucalyptus or larch are planted to provide the wood.

Thousands of logs are transported to pulp-mills by water, road or rail.

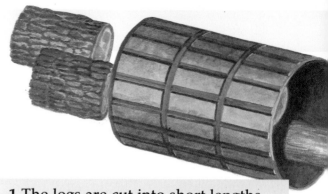

1 The logs are cut into short lengths. They are dropped into spinning drums which remove the bark.

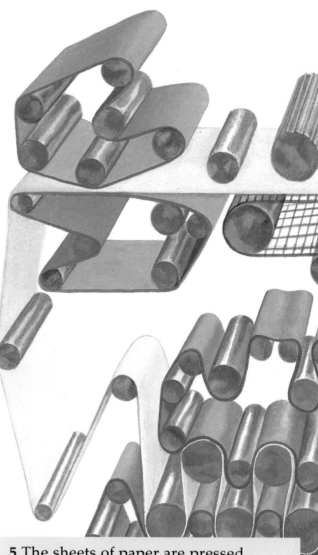

5 The sheets of paper are pressed between rollers and then dried. Finishing rollers make the surface of the paper smooth.

A paper mill in Canada

3 Various chemicals are added to the pulp to give it strength and colour. A substance called size is also added. This makes the paper partially waterproof so that it doesn't soak up the ink.

2 The stripped logs are then made into a pulp. This is done mechanically by mashing them or by adding chemicals. A lot of water is used at this stage.

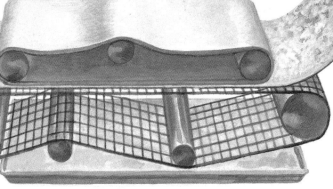

4 The pulp is spread out on to a very fine wire mesh. Most of the water drains away. The fibres of the wood bind together to form sheets of paper.

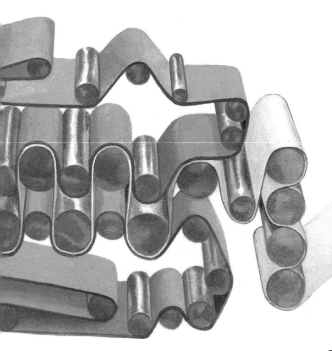

Rolls of paper before cutting

Folklore and religion

Trees play an important part in many of the world's religions, and in the stories people tell and the customs they follow. This may be because they grow larger and live longer than other living things. Since the earliest times, trees have helped to sustain and enhance human life.

Sacred tree

Buddhists follow the teaching of the Buddha who died about 483 BC. He is said to have become enlightened, or gained wisdom in all things, while sitting under a tree. A sapling of this tree still grows in Sri Lanka today. It is sacred to Buddhists.

Trees in our language

You can see how important trees are to us by studying the things we say. There are many sayings which refer to trees. To 'branch out' means to work in new areas. To 'take root' means to stay in one place. A 'chip off the old block' is a young person who has the same characteristics as one of his or her parents; they are made of the same 'stuff'.

Tree places

Britain was once covered with trees. Many places are named after the old words for trees or forests. Places such as Oakley in Dorset and Ashbourne in Derbyshire were named after the trees that grew there. How many others can you find?

Oak worship

The druids were the teachers and religious leaders of the ancient Celtic peoples of Britain and Ireland. They worshipped trees, especially the oak, as part of their religion. The druids' rituals were carried out in sacred woodland groves or glades.

Famous oaks

There are many famous oaks in Britain. Fascinating stories are attached to them, but they may not always be true! Robin Hood's Larder was a 1000-year-old oak in Sherwood Forest, Nottinghamshire. It is said that the outlaw hid his food in its hollow trunk.

World tree

Yggdrasil is the world tree of Scandinavian mythology. It is believed that the tree binds together heaven, Earth and hell with its roots and branches.

Banyan tree

Banyan trees are sacred to Hindus of India. These trees support the weight of their spreading branches with pillar roots. There are stories from ancient times of whole armies sheltering beneath banyan trees.

An ancient Banyan tree; the second oldest in India

Trading trees and planting gardens

Trees have been traded between countries for centuries. At first the trade was in fruit trees such as apricots, lemons and peaches. Many ancient civilizations traded and planted trees to make gardens for people to enjoy.

Moving in with trees

In the past, conquering civilizations brought their trees to the countries they moved into. The ancient Greeks took olive trees to Italy and Sicily, where they have become an important food crop. The Romans brought sweet chestnuts to Britain.

Planting in rows

Ways of planting trees in gardens go in and out of fashion just like styles of clothes or buildings. In the eighteenth century, plants were grown in neat rows and the design was very symmetrical; these were known as formal gardens.

An Italian olive grove

Back to nature

In the latter half of the eighteenth century, people started to plant gardens that looked more natural. Capability Brown designed many of these, including the one pictured on the right. He never saw the gardens how he had imagined them because it takes a hundred years or more for many of the trees to become fully grown.

A formal garden in Gloucestershire, England

A Capability Brown garden in Wiltshire, England

The tree collectors

During the fifteenth and sixteenth centuries, European gardeners became very excited about new plants being discovered in the Americas. They sent people out to these lands to collect seeds and seedlings.

The Douglas fir is now common in Britain. Seeds of this species were collected in North America and brought to Britain in 1825 by a collector called David Douglas. Instead of cutting down the tree to get the seeds, Douglas used to shoot down the cones.

Landscape favourite

The monkey puzzle tree is a pine from Chile in South America. A small number of seeds were first sent to Britain in 1797. There were very few monkey puzzle trees at first but many gardeners wanted them. When more seeds arrived, the tree became very fashionable among Victorian gardeners.

Preserving the forests

There are few natural and ancient forests in Europe today. Most of the trees we see were planted by someone for a reason. In the past, some forests were preserved so that a few rich and powerful people could hunt in them. Trespassers were dealt with harshly. Today, many are preserved for everyone to enjoy.

Planting today

Planting trees on a large scale needs careful planning. The young trees must be protected as they grow. It is important for local wildlife that they are the right kind of trees.

Fast-growing money

Softwoods such as pine and spruce are a valuable crop because they grow quickly. Unfortunately, closely packed plantations of these trees prevent the sunlight from reaching the ground below and nothing else can grow. They are not good places for wildlife.

A softwood plantation

Protecting the young

Young, newly planted trees are protected from hungry animals by plastic tubes. They are planted in neat rows so that it is easy to clear unwanted plants that grow between them.

Mixed is best

Plantations of native trees make better habitats for wildlife than imported trees. Mixed woodland, with many different kinds of tree, is less likely to be wiped out by disease than a plantation of just one kind.

Trees in the landscape

The fact that people plant trees wherever they settle may be because wooded landscapes are more friendly than barren, treeless ones.

Living in the city

Plane trees are often planted in cities because they can put up with pollution better than most trees. Gingkoes are also very popular in built-up areas.

Kew Gardens, London, England in the autumn

Natural shields

Trees are used to hide large buildings such as factories. They make the surroundings more pleasant for the people who work in these buildings.

Trees help to cut out noise from busy roads. They are also planted on the steep banks beside motorways to keep the soil in place. A group of trees around a house forms a shelter from the wind.

Many French roads are lined with trees.

An avenue of trees in France

Park design

When parks are planted they are also designed. Trees of different shapes and colours are planted next to each other to give variety. The trees bloom and their leaves change colour at different times of the year.

Gingko tree in a city park

41

Losing the trees

Most of the natural forests of Europe were cut down a long time ago. Small areas have been replaced. The rain forests are being cut down today. They cannot be replaced. There are many reasons why the forests are being cut down, and some important reasons why they shouldn't be.

Why the forests are cut down

Timber production Hardwood from the rain forests makes a lot of money for countries who need it badly. Unfortunately, the money will run out because new trees are not planted to replace the old ones. Every year 20.4 million hectares of forest are cut down.

Stacking logs that were once part of a rain forest in the Philippines

Cattle ranches Rain forests are cleared to make land for cattle to graze on.

New farming areas The people who clear the forests for timber make roads. People from other parts of the country follow these roads and make their homes in new areas of forest. They clear the land for farming. Unfortunately, there are too many new settlers and they clear too much forest.

Why we need the forests

1 Trees and plants produce oxygen when they make their food. All living things need oxygen to survive.

2 Trees help to reduce the amount of CO_2 in the air.

3 The rain forests contain a huge variety of plant and animal life that lives nowhere else. If the forests are cut down, all this will be lost.

4 Many thousands of people live in the rain forests and will be homeless without them.

5 The roots of trees bind the soil together. When the trees are removed, the soil is easily washed or blown away. Nothing can grow when this happens, not even grass for cattle.

6 Trees soak up water from the soil. They release much of it back into the air through their leaves. When trees are cut down, this water just runs away. Without this water crops cannot grow.

Poisoning the trees

Trees killed by acid rain

Just like us, forests need clean air to survive. They also help to clean the air. When we lose our trees we lose a vital part of our planet's 'air conditioning machinery'.

Acid rain

The forests of temperate countries are also dying. Poisonous fumes are produced by cars, factories and power stations, usually when they burn fossil fuels such as coal and oil. These fumes mix with water in the air to make acid rain. Acid rain poisons the soil and kills trees. It also pollutes lakes and rivers.

Pollution on the move

Acid rain can be carried a long way by the wind before it falls as rain or snow.
- Every year, 3.3 million tonnes of acid pollution is blown into Canada from the USA.
- The rain that falls on European countries today contains 80 times as much acid as it did 40 years ago.

The greenhouse effect

Trees and plants help to absorb CO_2 from the air. Carbon dioxide acts like the glass in a greenhouse; it traps heat.

Without trees and plants, the Earth will heat up. This will create new deserts and raise the water level of the oceans, causing catastrophic floods.

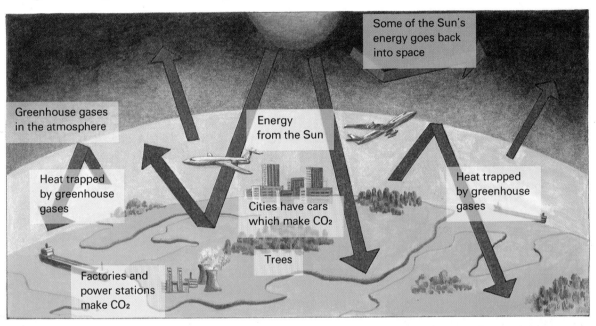

Some of the Sun's energy goes back into space

Greenhouse gases in the atmosphere

Energy from the Sun

Heat trapped by greenhouse gases

Heat trapped by greenhouse gases

Cities have cars which make CO_2

Trees

Factories and power stations make CO_2

Possible solutions to acid rain

To prevent acid rain, people and organizations which cause pollution should clean up their act.

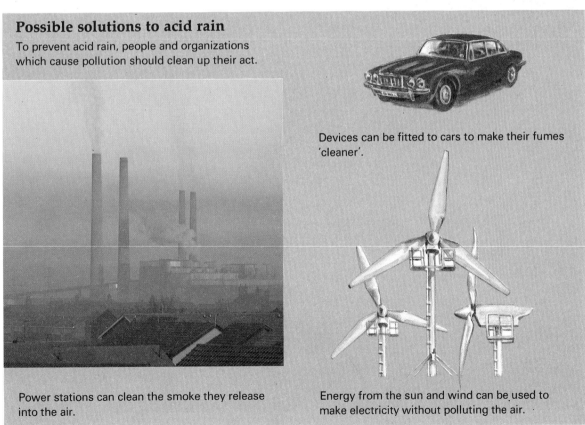

Devices can be fitted to cars to make their fumes 'cleaner'.

Power stations can clean the smoke they release into the air.

Energy from the sun and wind can be used to make electricity without polluting the air.

Save our trees

We need trees to survive. The problems facing the forests are large and complex, but not impossible to solve. There are many things that can be done, even by people who live a long way from the forests that are being lost.

Firewood plantations

In countries where firewood is scarce, areas of fast-growing trees can be planted for this purpose. When trees are cut down, new ones should be planted.

Stoves, not fires

People living in parts of Kenya have recently started cooking their food on stoves rather than open fires. Stoves lose less heat to the open air. They use less wood, and so help to save trees.

Safe homes

Nature reserves and national parks provide safe homes for plants and animals. They should be looked after by visitors and people who live near them. Tourists visiting the parks bring money into countries that need it.

Planting plans

In countries where the forests have gone, new ones can be planted. This will prevent the soil being washed away, or eroded. New planting schemes are under way in Costa Rica, Kenya, Vietnam, China and Brazil.

Workers planting out tree seedlings in Nepal

Hugging trees

In India, there is a forest that was saved because the women hugged the trees. This stopped the tree fellers cutting them down. In other parts of the world, people have done similar things to protect trees.

The man who planted trees

There is a popular story in France about a shepherd called Elzeard Bouffier who is known as 'the man who planted trees and grew happiness'. Every day, for many years, he planted seeds until a forest stood where he had worked. Although this is just a story, we should try to follow his example.

Take action to save trees

Here's what you can do:

1 Use less energy in the house. Turn off unnecessary lights. By using less energy, we use less fossil fuels which damage the environment. This will cut down on acid rain.

2 Travel on foot or by bike, instead of by car. Encourage people to share car journeys. This will cut down on pollution.

3 Take your rubbish, especially paper, to recycling points. This will cut down on the number of trees felled.

4 Look after the woodlands you visit.

5 Buy recycled paper products.

6 Do not buy products made from rain forest wood.

7 Find out how to plant seeds or saplings, then go out and do it, or join a group and work with them.

Index

*Numbers in **bold** indicate illustrations.*

Published by BBC Educational Publishing,
a division of BBC Enterprises Ltd,
Woodlands, 80 Wood Lane, London W12 0TT

First published 1993
© Andrew Charman/BBC Enterprises Ltd 1993
The moral rights of the author have been asserted.

Paperback ISBN: 0 563 35017 2
Hardback ISBN: 0 563 35018 0
Typeset by Ace Filmsetting Ltd, Frome, Somerset
Colour reproduction by Daylight Colour, Singapore
Cover origination in England by Dot Gradations
Printed and bound by BPCC, Paulton

Photo Credits
Ardea **pages 9** R walker, **37** J Van Gruisen, **44** Wolfshead/B Osborne; Bodleian Library, Oxford **page 2** *MS Ouseley Add 176 folio 311 verso*; The Bridgeman Art Library/Whitford & Hughes, London **page 27 (bottom)**; J Allan Cash Ltd **page 26 (bottom)**; Bruce Colman Ltd **pages 4** G Dore, **7** L L Rue III, **12/13** G D Plage, **18** R P Carr, **24 (top right)** G McCarthy, **25 (top left)**, **27 (top)**, **33** M P L Fogden, **41 (top)** J Cowan; Ecoscene **page 35** S Morgan; The Environmental Picture Library **pages 21** A McCarthy, **23 (bottom)** P Sutherland, **28** H Girardet, **34**, **42 (top)** A Olah, **45** S Gamester, **46**; Mary Evans Picture Library **pages 24 (top left and bottom left)**; The Garden Picture Library **pages 38 (bottom)** C Boursnell, **39** J Bethell; Robert Harding Picture Library **pages 20**, **24 (bottom right)**, **25 (bottom)**; Michael Holford **page 22**; Holt Studios **pages 38 (top)**, **40** N Cattlin; Hutchison Library **page 31** R Francis; Institute of Agricultural History and Museum of English Rural Life, University of Reading **page 25 (top right)**; Panos Pictures **page 30** J Hammond & N Cooper; Picturepoint Ltd **page 23 (top)**; Still Pictures **page 42 (bottom)** M Edwards; Zefa **pages 3**, **29**.

Front cover: Zefa **(main picture)**, Science Photo Library **(bottom right)**.

Illustrations © Philip Hood 1992